D1273826

SUELLEN SNYDER
Anshe Slonim, Norfolk Street,
Oldest Synagogue in New York City

following page
DEBBIE LEAVITT
Brian, Santa Barbara

Behold
a
Great
Image

the contemporary Jewish experience in photographs
edited by **Sharon Strassfeld** and **Arthur Kurzweil**
introduction by Arthur A. Cohen
designed by Adrianne Onderdonk Dudden

The Jewish Publication Society of America · Philadelphia 5738-1978

*Because all of the photographers have donated their work to this book,
and because all profits from the sale of this book will be going to tzedakah,
we dedicate this volume to the commandment of giving. As Rabbi Assi observed:
"Tzedakah is as important as all the other commandments put together."*

Photographers / page numbers of their works

Copyright © 1978 by Sharon Strassfeld and Arthur Kurzweil
"Sights, Images, and Photographs," Copyright © 1978
by Arthur A. Cohen.
First edition   All rights reserved
ISBN 0-8276-0105-0
Library of Congress catalog card no. 78-1168
Manufactured in the United States of America

The editors wish to thank the following publishers for
permission to reprint from the sources listed: Bloch
Publishing Co., for "This Etrog Is an Etrog," from Rejoice in
Thy Festival: A Treasury of Wisdom, Wit and Humor for the
Sabbath and Jewish Holidays by Philip Goodman; Holt,
Rinehart and Winston, Publishers, for The Gates of the Forest
by Elie Wiesel, translated by Frances Frenaye; Department
of Youth Activities, United Synagogue of America, for: "A
Recent Immigrant Comes from the Soviet Union to His
Family in the U. S." and "Hebrew" from And God Braided
Eve's Hair by Danny Siegel.

אלו צלם חד שגיא

BEHOLD A GREAT IMAGE Daniel 2:31

בצלם אלהים
IN HIS IMAGE

בין אדם למקום
PARTNERSHIP

ישראל
ISRAEL, THE LAND

May He who blessed our fathers Abraham, Isaac, and Jacob, and our mothers Sarah, Rivkah, Leah, and Rachel bless
Adrianne Onderdonk Dudden, whose artistic talent and creative design guided this book from idea to publication
Maier Deshell, who saw our vision and pursued it with us
Roman Vishniac and Susan T. Goodman, who plowed through the multitude of photographs and helped us to find the best
The Association of Tzedakah Collectives, who provided the prize money for the Contest and the spirit of giving to which this book is dedicated
Michael Strassfeld and Lisa Kurzweil, for reasons they know—and much more
Maris Engel, for the publicity poster she designed for the Contest and for her constant dedication to purpose
Mark Nulman, who is miraculously always there when he is needed
Bill Kavesh, Judy Hauptman, Debby Mowshowitz, Beth Levine, and David Szonyi, for their extra special assistance
Wolfe Kelman and Laura Schwab of the Rabbinical Assembly
Daniel Syme of the Union of American Hebrew Congregations
And the photographers, for their patience, support, and most of all their talent

Editors' Preface

A Bit of History In the spring of 1975, a group of young American Jews, the present editors among them, gathered at Weiss' Farm, a retreat house in New Jersey, to consider the issue of *tzedakah*. Underlying our discussion was the awareness that the term *tzedakah*, generally translated as "charity," derives from the Hebrew root *tzedek*, "justice"—a connotation that lends an entirely different emphasis to the activity, indeed the *mitzvah*, of *tzedakah*. All of us believed that *tzedakah* must not be regarded as a mere act of voluntary generosity; *tzedakah*, we affirmed, in accord with Jewish tradition, is to be seen as an obligation imposed by Jewish law.

At Weiss' Farm we also considered our own personal estrangement from the American Jewish fund-raising establishment. This had come about from our observation of the realities of Jewish fund-raising and -disbursement practice in the United States. For all the huge amounts of money raised by the local Jewish federations, presumably collected from a broad base of donors, the fact is that a disproportionately large share of the funds is contributed by a small percentage of Jews, the so-called "big-givers." These, in turn—this is certainly true in the large cities—often dictate how the funds are to be allocated. Thus, because of the priorities established by the affluent minority, many deserving institutions and groups of individuals remain underfunded, or even unfunded. Wide sectors of Jews, including the elderly, students, the handicapped, the poor, women, and artists, receive no communal funds at all and are unrepresented by the very bodies that claim to speak for the American Jewish community.

Noting all this, a decision was taken to found groups to be known as Tzedakah Collectives. Their members, we agreed, would contribute their *tzedakah* money to the collectives that would then, in a democratic manner, make allocations consistent with the beliefs and attitudes of their members. And so the first Tzedakah Collectives came into being. Before long there were groups in Philadelphia, Boston, Washington, New York, Los Angeles, and Cleveland.

The Contest In the course of time, one of the New York collectives—the Derech Reut (Path of Friendship) Tzedakah Collective—began to explore the idea of extending its activities beyond the range of more conventional "giving." The hope was to make a contribution to the community of another kind—less tangible, perhaps, but no less important—one that might accommodate certain areas of communal neglect, specifically, culture, education, and the arts. What was called for, it seemed, were projects that would attend to the largely unattended aspects of American Jewish life. Such projects, were they to be developed, would also serve to draw into the orbit of the community's concern the host of untapped and unaffiliated talent that is known to abound "out there."

One suggestion, no doubt prompted by the increased interest in photography as an art form, was to sponsor a photography contest for amateur photographers that would reflect aspects of the contemporary Jewish experience. Apart from the intrinsic value of the effort—a visual exploration, however incomplete, of current Jewish moods—the contest, it was felt, would also draw out (and draw in) hitherto unknown Jewish talents. All this could only enrich the spirit of the community as a whole.

The proposal to hold a photography contest was readily adopted. Other Tzedakah Collectives were invited to cooperate in the enterprise; joining Derech Reut were the collectives of the Washington Fabrangen and the Boston Havurah. The editors of this volume—members of Derech Reut—volunteered to administer the contest; rules were drawn up; a poster announcing the contest was designed and widely distributed. The three collectives in association assumed the obligation to provide the prize money for the winners-to-be. Graciously agreeing to serve as judges were Roman Vishniac, the distinguished photographer, and Susan T. Goodman, curator of The Jewish Museum in New York.

The response was overwhelming, exceeding all expectations. By the time of the deadline date, more than 1,000 entries had been received. The judges then met to consider the bounty. Their choices—which, of course, appear in this book—were:

FIRST PRIZE: Suellen Snyder *Zitomer Yeshiva, New York City, Stripped Interior*
SECOND PRIZE: Bill Aron *New York Havurah School*
THIRD PRIZE: Irving I. Herzberg *Hanukkah Candles*
HONORABLE MENTION: Carl Bianco *Caskets, Sinai*
    Isaac Geld *Former Synagogue*
    Rhyna Goldsmith *Broom Seller*
    Adam Baruch Laipson *"The Tower," Sculpture by Kenneth Snelson, Hirshhorn Museum, Washington*
    Mordechai Meles *Salute to Israel Parade, New York City*
    Shimon Morali *Meah Shearim*
    Karen Pliskin *Lady of Shiraz*
    Benjamin S. Rosen *Brother and Sister, Jerusalem*
    Fred Rosenberg *Grove Street Cemetery, Newark*
    Sy Rubin *Purim Masquerade, Brooklyn*

The Book Early in the proceedings, while the contest was still a glimmer in the minds of the sponsors, it occurred to us that the best entries, those of special merit and interest, might very well make up a book, to provide a permanent record for the community. Accordingly, The Jewish Publication Society of America was approached and found to be agreeable to the idea. Accruing royalties from the sale of the book, it was decided, would be turned over to a committee of representatives from the three Tzedakah Collectives, who jointly would allocate the monies to other Jewish educational and cultural projects.

Heartened by the prospect of publication, the administrators of the contest now became editors as well. Shaping this book—finding the form that would best contain the collective vision of its many "eyes"—was for us an exhilarating experience. Most of all, it afforded an opportunity to share in the creativity of its true creators, the photographers from far and wide who sought to capture one or another facet of the variegated Jewish experience of our day. We trust that the aim of both contest and book—to hold up a mirror to a vibrant Jewish actuality—has been handsomely accomplished. Here, to our minds, is indeed an incomparable collection of great Jewish images. We hope that you, the viewers and readers, will agree, and we bid you, behold!

Finally, we hope, too, that the impulse that brought this book to light has in some measure been realized: to impart a new sense of *tzedakah* to American Jewish life, one that might bring together the whole community in work for the good of the community. In the words of Rabbi Yohanan the sandalmaker (Ethics of the Fathers 4:14): "Every assembly which is in the name of Heaven will in the end endure." Amen, selah!

Sharon Strassfeld / *Arthur Kurzweil*

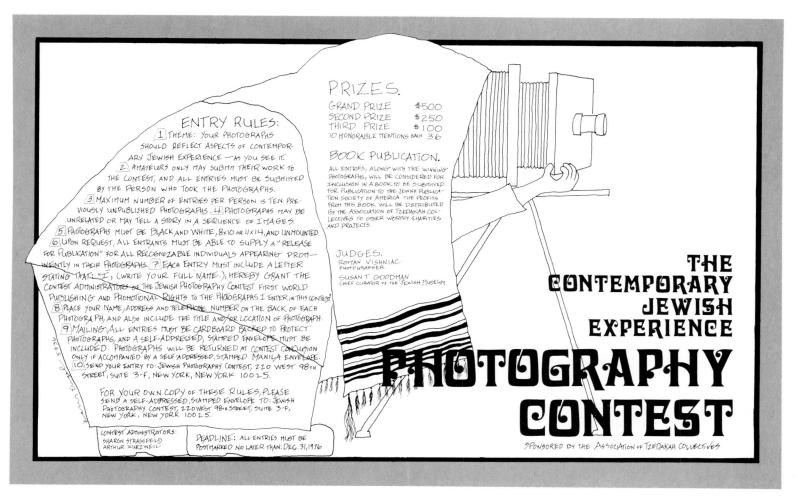

MARIS ENGEL
Photo Contest Poster

Introduction / Sight, Images, and Photographs
Arthur A. Cohen

The photographic images before us exist in five-fold removal from the flow of the real. The river of reality that Heraclitus, philosopher of ancient Ephesus, regarded as the metaphor of underlying change cannot be photographed. The photographer lays over the flow an eye of perception (an aperture shaped and widened, like the soul, with conditions and determinants matured in the shallows of the unconscious) and interposes between them a device loaded with paper sensitized to light. The flowing real is caught in a squint and the image, traced upon a rectangle of paper, is sequestered from light until removed and bathed. Already the image is twice-removed from the real—eye, box before eye, triggering the boxed eye, seeing through the eyed box—until it is registered. The everflowing real is now frozen by the camera, an artificial extension of the eye, itself linked by a complex neurological machinery to the brain. The river of the real; the light that swathes it; the box that focuses it; the eye that frames it; the brain that shapes the will to see and forms the decision to make the image—all these fix a cut of the real. Only the box, after all, is unique to making the photograph. The remainder of the procedure is as millennially ancient in the evolution of the species as the seeing eye itself.

The box before the eye is not alone the history of a technique and process, but a process and technique of history—a way of making an assertion about history, arresting and employing a selection, and a framing of the real in such a way as to command an attitude and ultimately to enforce a judgment. This fact arises not so much from the relation that is thought to exist between photography and art, the former suggesting the illusion of being real (replicating the real in flat accuracy), while painting depends upon the reality of the illusion. Rather, it is a convenient way of describing the general assumption about the relation of arts and pseudo-arts, between the artistocracy of some arts, and the proleterian employment of mechanical reproductive arts.

The current view that photography, like lithography, film, and phonograph recording, is an instrumentality of late capitalism, manipulated for the democratization (read, as well, routinization and distribution) of aristocratic culture, removing the aesthetic object from the private transaction of patron and artist, has the advantage of supplying photography with a context within egalitarian culture, while making the error of supposing that the art of previous cultures, admittedly sacred or hieratic

7

or elitist, was also without vital, indeed primary, connection to the imagination. This unfortunate consequence of an insufficiently critical response to Walter Benjamin's seminal investigation of the vulgarization of art (or, more accurately, the stripping from art of its "aura," its numinal patina) in this age of mechanical reproduction,* results in part from the fact that Benjamin's essay is tied to an essentially sociological assessment of technical means; in part to the enforced limitation of Benjamin's frame of reference; and in part to the commonplace, but no less inaccurate, transposition of criteria derived from a profound knowledge of literature to the visual arts (an intellectual version of the biologist's ratamorphic fallacy), where his familiarity and sensibility remained essentially literary and consequently inappropriate. The principal issue that emerges from the mounting comment and extension of Benjamin's thesis is the inability to address the imagination except in terms of its cultural environment, the ethos of avarice in capitalist society, or the formal means of making and producing art objects or, finally, the narrative, linear, expository intention of arts deprived of their plasticity by reproduction. The absence of consideration given the imagination, of course, evidences the disengagement of criticism from the centers of autonomy and privacy, but it also entails the withdrawal from the critical sensibility of those principles by which to connect the made with the interior process of making, and the history of art from the theory of the imagination, in effect, the final divorce, threatened since the end of the last century, between the imagination and the theory of knowledge.

We are left—post-Benjamin natus—with artifacts, the detritus of the imagination, and from these we are expected to form our notions of art and its history. How perverse an enterprise!

The issue of the imagination returns us to the question of photography and the photographic book.

A photographic book is not simply a book of photographs—a mere collection of images, each discrete and lonely, uninvolved in the sequence of images. During the thirties the annual, Photographie, appeared in France; very similar to, although less journalistically preoccupied than, U. S. Camera or the German Europa-Camera, Photographie came close to the notion of a book of photographs. Subjects were identified—the nude, the city, the sea, technology, random subjects selected by the clustering of excellent images rather than by editorial requirement. Where splendid photographs by Gidal, Moholy-Nagy, Rodchenko, Bayer would gather there would be cityscapes; Man Ray, Kertesz, Brassaï would tell of night life; Bruehl, George Platt Lynes, Biermann, Beaton, striking heads and bodies. In other words, the photographs composed the subject matter, defined the editorial sensibility, and often supplied nothing more than page after page of disparate and marvelously printed gravure reproductions of great images.

U.S. Camera, however, was different. Photo-journalism, which we popularly associate with Life magazine, Sunday-supplement photography of earlier days, is essentially story-telling photography in which the concern is not the medium, but the information. The photographer told stories or, like ancient sculptors described by Lessing, the eighteenth-century German humanist, in his Laocoön, identified the image in its rictus and closed the shutter (Capa's photograph of the wounded Spanish Loyalist falling backwards into death), seizing and prizing in penultimacy before consummating in collapse, pulverization, explosion, or death. Lessing's classical notion of sculpture as the art that implies time by freezing space in a single moment has come to truth again as photography; the very terms we employ for the relationship between

camera eye and object are essentially out of Lessing—trap, freeze, seize, catch, and arrest all suggest an act of holding the object at a particular instant, obliging it to stand still before its end, before it falls (bomb or body), hits (bullet or punch), or before it comes to earth and settles into the various attitudes of crumpling and dying. Photo-journalism, in its narrative passion, is then like sculpture, suggesting the possibilities of catastrophe and tragedy and the ordinary drama of modern life.

The photographic periodicals that disseminated the craft of photography were concerned with amateur mimesis—"You, too, can take terrific photographs, just like Weegee or Walker Evans or Ben Shahn or Dorothea Lange; you can tell us about the poverty-brutality-cruelty-violence of American life and we'll publish and pay you for it; but remember, please, the shutter speed and which film you used and, of course, the camera make, the machine, the equipment complex that fed your craft (and feeds the whole photographic industry)." Nobody made money out of taking photographs until very recently, not the photographers, not the book publishers, and not the editors of books and periodicals.

The photographic book has come of age.

The photographic book can be a sequence of images without words (not photography as illustration to text, like Steichen's photographs for Thoreau's Walden or Edward Weston's for Whitman's Leaves of Grass, which have virtually no functional difference than that of gloss, commentary, addendum to the primary text), the photographs organized by a single sensibility, displaying the skin and texture of a reality, evoking its light and grayness, its scaliness and shabby exterior, its grotesquerie, its folly, its grandeur no less (Paul Strand's Time in New England, Bernice Abbott's Changing New York, Brassaï's Paris de Nuit, Wright Morris's The Inhabitant, or Clarence John Laughlin's Ghosts Along the Mississippi). Or there is the photographic book which is the omnium gatherum of a single ego, an omnivore of eye that eats and digests everything (Cartier-Bresson's France, David Douglas Duncan's Yankee Nomad); or the work which consecrates a thematic single-mindedness, indifferent to the text which is motivated by other considerations and attitudes (Moholy-Nagy's sixty-four photographs for Benedetta's The Street Markets of London or Walker Evans's photographs for James Agee's Let Us Now Praise Famous Men).

All of these, unremarkably, are not simply anthologies of photographs, but selections in the act of photographing; that is, the photographer has made a choice before taking the photograph. However much he may ultimately select from a hundred versions of a single subject, there was—before the act—a greater or lesser intelligence making critical judgment. This procedure is even more exaggerated today when the technology of the camera has reached the point where it becomes possible to shoot thousands of photographs in the same time that it took Atget—the French photographer of empty Parisian streets and shops (what Benjamin called the scenes of crime)—to shoot a single photograph. The fast camera promotes fast sight, yielding place of sensibility to editorial opinion, quite literally, to snapshot (as in "snap judgment"). The great Civil War photographer, Matthew Brady, could photograph the dead, the immobile wounded, the posing generals, but he could not—as we—photograph the trajectory of the bullet.

The photographic book before me, Behold a Great Image, is something else again, not quite a new genre, but grounded in a premise of anthology not widely employed. The editors have judged a competition among hundreds of entrant photographers, all presumably challenged to reflect visions of a single order of life. The judges chose what in their view were the best photographs. The photographs demanded an organization to be made into a book, a book which would narrate with affection

*Walter Benjamin, "The Work of Art in the Age of Mechanical Reproduction," Illuminations: Essays and Reflections, New York, 1968.

and warmth the appeal and sympathy of contemporary Jewish life. It is a handsome volume, intensified by an almost liturgic repetitiveness, one image complementing and reinforcing the next. It is a volume that raises questions, not unrelated to those with which I began.

Clearly, single photographic images can be iconic, characterizing more than themselves, evoking times and sensibilities, coming by repetition and use, frequency of presentation and variety of context to suggest and stand for the whole, ultimately, as direct recollection fails, to replace the whole. The capped child with arms upraised, yellow star pinned to his overcoat, the Nazi soldier behind him with pointing gun—this is the Warsaw ghetto, but it is now so much more as well; the Frenchman weeping as the German army parades in conquest through Paris—another image become liturgical. Images such as the aforementioned are parts that suggest and imply the whole; they replace the whole; they become the whole. It is not, of course, as it should be. A persecuted boy or a weeping Frenchman should not displace the complex reality that is so much more. But it is in the nature of photography in popular culture (in culture proleterianized and demystified) that its images should become iconic, condensing a whole world of history and experience into, for instance, an old woman's eye-glassed eye shattered by a Cossack bullet.

The single image replaces a whole world of events, whole histories and the requirements of memory. Do you imagine that the historian, Simon Dubnow, murdered by a militiaman in Nazi-occupied Riga in 1941 would have said: "Photograph this scene!" Not at all. He called out to memory; he urged that the mind photograph, print, store, and recall. The print of the mind is more assured than the photograph. To be sure, the photograph is permanence if the archivist in us all remembers to retrieve the image, but the print of memory—even if superficially banished from recollection by fear and anguish—is there throughout life to the borders of death.

It is then that *Behold a Great Image* should be regarded, as an anthology of suggestions to memory, an *aide-memoire*, an aleph-beth, a grammarian's syntax of Jewish life, full of delights and amusements, sorrows and sadnesses, dessuetude and atrophy, signs and wonders, refurbishments and final passings, each image serving as a kind of incitement to memory. The photograph shall never be the reality; it is not memory nor its replacement; it is not art nor even artifice; it is simply one eye, many eyes, looking through their own youthful lenses and finding what is both worth shuttering and shuddering, remembering and causing us to tremble.

I dislike nostalgia; I despise sentiment. It is untruth. The world is harder and more lean after all this time. I would have wished to find in this volume more abstraction, photographs of Hebrew letters, collages of reality, constructions which fueled the imagination rather than satiating it, but I understand why the editors eschewed such an option. In fact, it was not theirs to enjoy. They were the anthologists, but not the eyes. They selected the best from what they received and the best is very good indeed, as anyone examining *Behold a Great Image* will immediately recognize. It is more than nostalgic and more than sentimental; although the presence of these is palpable, there is, as well, the disarray of cemeteries and the despair of old people's homes and the bitter-sweetness of decay. The visions are various, but to have visionaries what is required is vastly more than a camera. A camera is, as we have said, merely an artifice interposed between the brain and the flow of the real. Educating the brain is a vaster enterprise than is learning to take beautiful pictures and that is why, perhaps, there are as few memorable photographers and photographs as there are artists like Cézanne and Matisse. But this is a cavil of my own hardness that should upset no one. What is written here is a comment on this volume and not an encomnium. *Behold a Great Image* is, after all, its own praise and celebration, needing none additional from me.

ALEX MERMEL
Shomer Shabbat

In His Image

בצלם אלהים

Faces

Male and female He created them   Genesis 1:27

זכר ונקבה ברא אתם

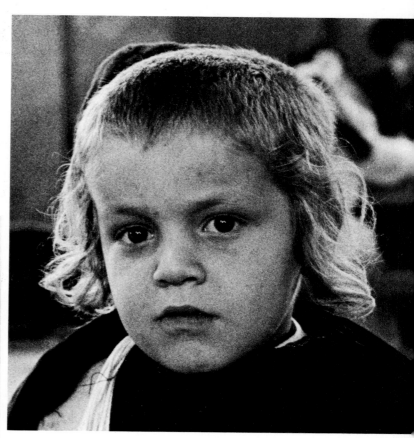

MORRIS M. FAIERSTEIN
Purim, Jerusalem

DENNIS BRISKIN
105-Year-Old Man, Arak, Iran

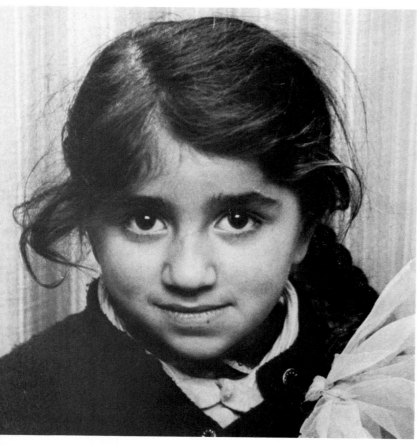

SHERRY SURIS
Young Soviet Immigrant

preceding pages
DEBBIE LEAVITT
Father and Son

BEA STADTLER
Yemenite Dancer

PHILIPPA GLAUBIGER
Young Hasid, Boston

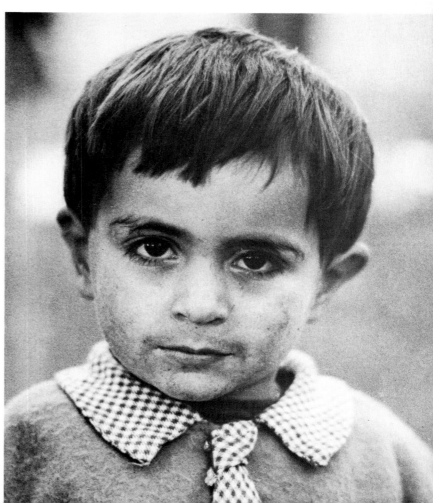

DENNIS BRISKIN
Persian Boy, Arak, Iran

EUGENE BLOCK
"Kissinger Wasn't That Bad"

EUGENE BLOCK
"Jimmy Carter Is Going to Win"

If God lived on earth, people would break His windows.   *Yiddish folksaying*

STEPHEN FOX
Shlomo Carlebach

IRVING I. HERZBERG
Old Man, Jerusalem

RICKI ROSEN
Two Matrons, Boro Park

16

RITA CATHERINE GRECO
Harry, Pittsburgh

SHELDON MOSKOWITZ
Child, Santa Barbara

IRVING I. HERZBERG
Moshe the Jeweler, Haifa

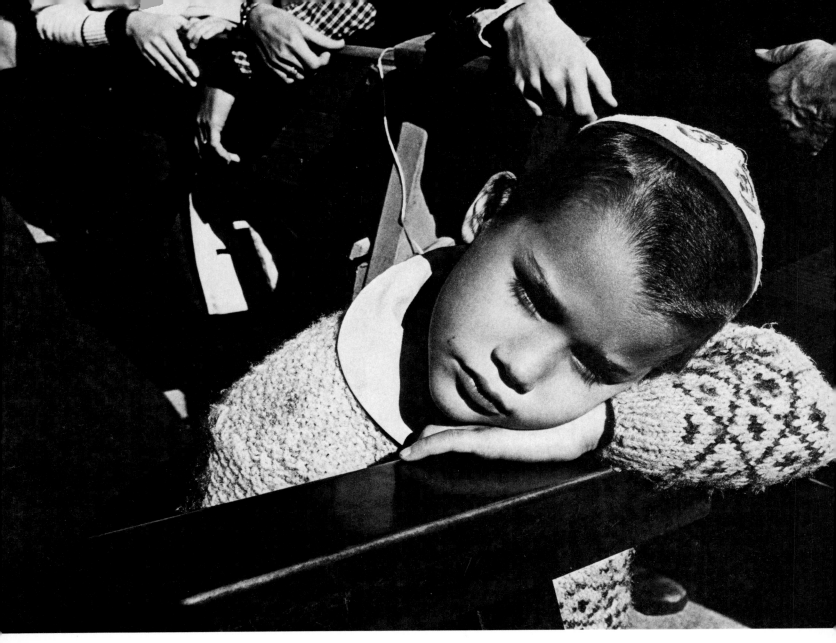

BILL ARON
On the Barricade, New York City

GARY H. POSNER
Grandmother, Baltimore

18

May the Lord grant strength to His people;
may the Lord bestow on His people well-being.   *Psalms 29:11*

below left
STANLEY NEWFIELD
Grand Rabbi Levi Horowitz, the Bostoner Rebbe

below
STEVEN YARINSKY
Hasidic Child, New York City

The Shekhinah rests on him who has a joyous heart.   *Jerusalem Talmud, Sukkah 5:1*

SHERRY SURIS
Reunion After 39 Years,
Russian Immigrant and Her Brother,
Lod Airport, 1972

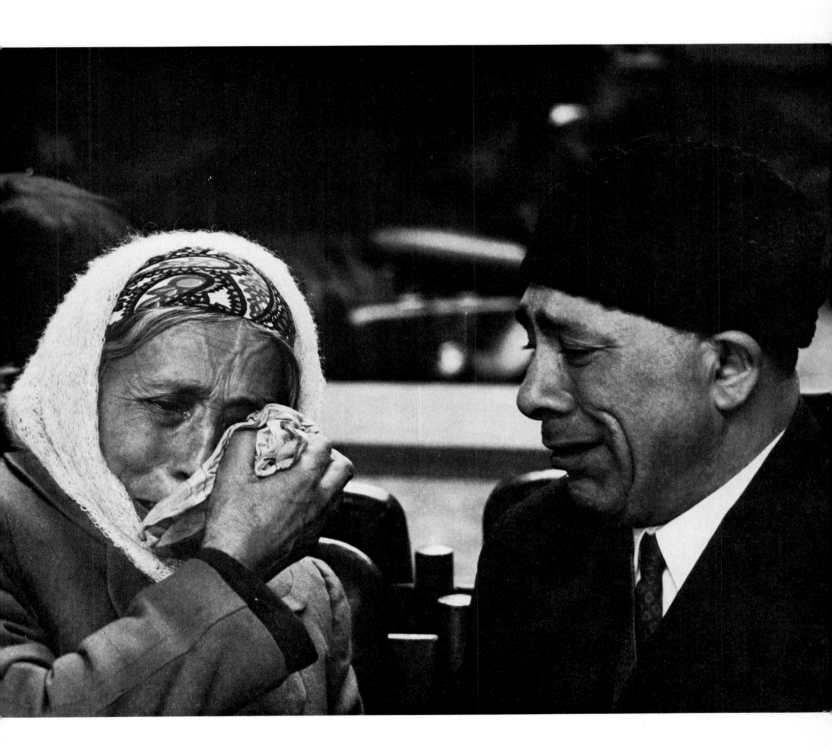

RICHARD B. MILLER
Visage

SHIMON MORALI
Portrait, Meah Shearim

To love God truly, one must first love man. If anyone tells you that he loves God
and does not love his fellow man, you will know that he is lying. *Hasidic saying*

Children

Let the father and the mother rejoice   Proverbs 23:25

ישמח אביך ואמך

ALVIN SILBERMAN
Kissing the Mezuzah

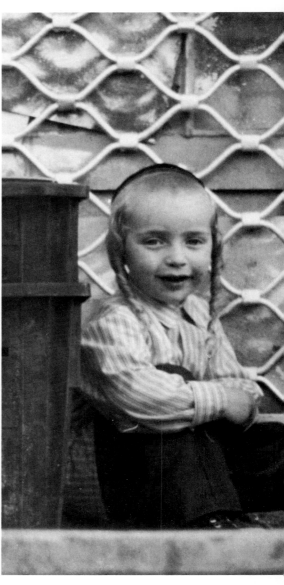

SURI LEVOW
Time Out, Jerusalem

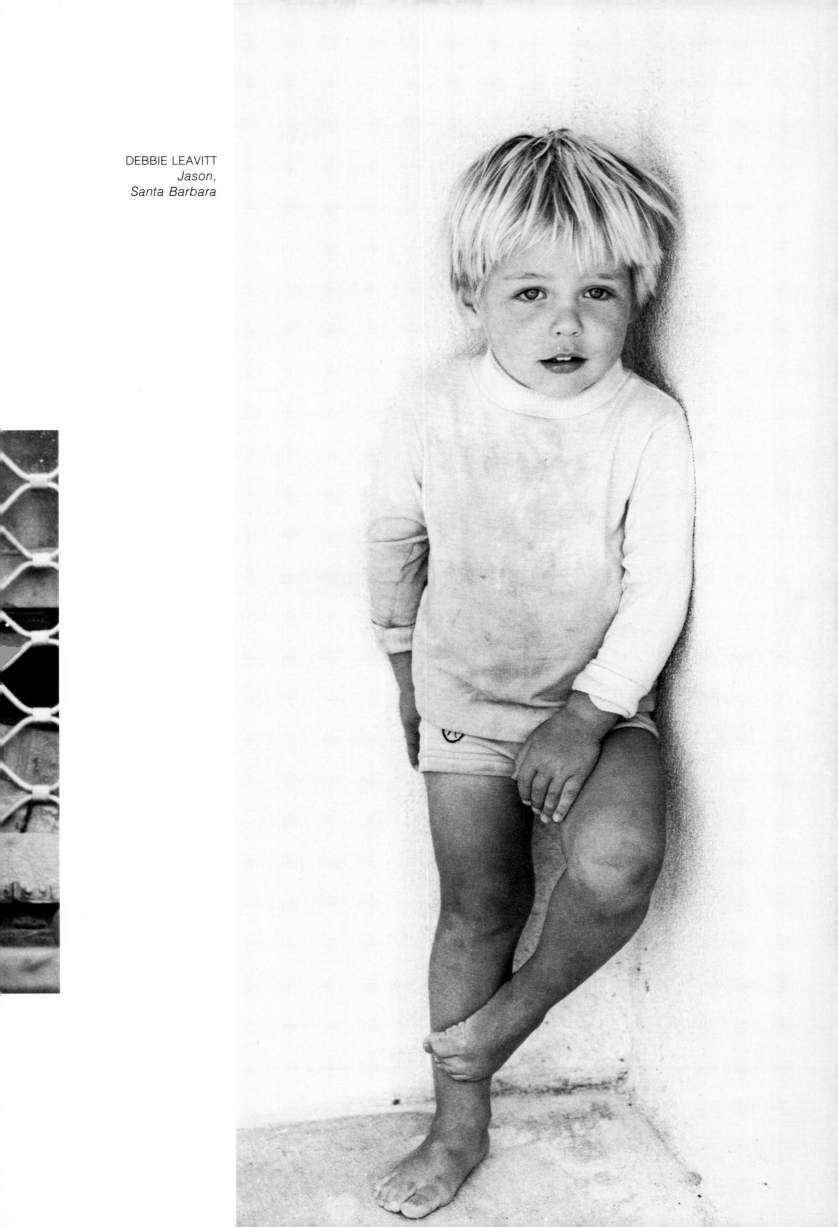

DEBBIE LEAVITT
*Jason,
Santa Barbara*

SHELDON MOSKOWITZ
Follow the Leader, Ezrat Torah Institute,
Goleta, California

SHELDON MOSKOWITZ
School Yard

JERRY SILVER
Yeshiva Bochers

STEPHEN FOX
Soviet Jewry Parade, New York City

27

SHELDON MOSKOWITZ
Classmates

SYLVIA VEGA-ORTIZ
In the Sinai Desert

AARON S. PEARLSTEIN
Dancers

The wolf shall dwell with the lamb,
The leopard lie down with the kid;
The calf, the beast of prey,
 and the fatling together,
With a little boy to herd them.

Isaiah 11:6

BENJAMIN S. ROSEN
Brother and Sister, Jerusalem
HONORABLE   MENTION

DAN FORBES
Great-Grandma

ZEVA OELBAUM
*Grandmother and
Grandchild, Kabul*

ETHEL DIAMOND
Shabbes Kiss

PHILIPPA GLAUBIGER
Father and Daughter

31

He was a friend. And what is a friend? More than a father, more than a brother; a traveling companion, with him you can conquer the impossible, even if you must lose it later. Friendship marks a life even more deeply than love. Friendship risks degenerating into obsession, friendship is never anything but sharing. It is to a friend that you communicate the awakening of a desire, the birth of a vision or a terror, the anguish of seeing the sun disappear or of finding that order and justice are no more. That's what you can talk about with a friend. Is the soul immortal, and if so why are we afraid to die? If God exists, how can we lay claim to freedom, since He is the beginning and its end? What is death, when you come down to it? The closing of a parenthesis, and nothing more? And what about life? In the mouth of a philosopher, these questions may have a false ring, but asked during adolescence or friendship, they have the power to change being: a look burns and ordinary gestures tend to transcend themselves. What is a friend? Someone who for the first time makes you aware of your loneliness and his, and helps you to escape so you in turn can help him. Thanks to him you can hold your tongue without shame and talk freely without risk. That's it.   Elie Wiesel, *Gates of the Forest*

ALVIN SILBERMAN
Twins, Long Beach, N. Y.

PETER A. COOPER
Brooklyn Boys

32

JERRY SILVER
Homeward Bound

JACKIE BIRNHAK
Hasidic Pair, Jerusalem

When Rabbi Noah the son of Rabbi Mordecai assumed the succession after the death of his father, his disciples noticed that there were a number of ways in which he conducted himself differently from his father. They asked him about this and he replied, "I do just as my father did. He did not imitate and I do not imitate." *Hasidic Tale*

GILLY SAFDEYE
Friends, Brooklyn

ZEVA OELBAUM
Friends, Jerusalem

Elderly

Moses' eyes were undimmed and his vigor unabated
Deuteronomy 34:7

לא כהתה עינו ולא נס לחה

DEBBIE LEAVITT
Pelta, Chicago

LINDA HARRIS
Tenement Window, Lower East Side

STUART FISHELSON
Two Women, Brooklyn

DAN FORBES
"I Have Considered the Days"

HARRIET LEIBOWITZ
The Latest News, Israel

KAREN PLISKIN
Lady of Shiraz
HONORABLE MENTION

40

WARREN SOLODAR
Bus Stop, Jerusalem

RHYNA GOLDSMITH
Venturing Forth, Jerusalem

HARRIET LEIBOWITZ
Pedestrians, Jerusalem

41

OPHERA HALLIS
Zaide 1

OPHERA HALLIS
Zaide 2

42

Gauge a country's prosperity by its treatment of the aged. Rabbi Nahman of Bratslav

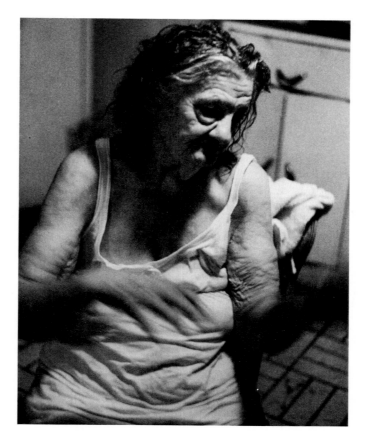

RICKI ROSEN
Sonya, Brighton Beach

CAROL BLOOM
Mother and Daughter

Honor your father and mother, even as you honor God, for all three were partners in your creation.   *Zohar*

BILL ARON
Grand Concourse 1

BILL ARON
Grand Concourse 2

If old men tell you "throw down" and young men tell you "build up," throw down and do not build up, because destruction by the old is construction, and construction by the young is often destruction. *Babylonian Talmud, Megillah 31a*

RICKI ROSEN
Conversation, Brighton Beach

CAROL BLOOM
Family Gathering 1

CAROL BLOOM
Family Gathering 2

RICKI ROSEN
On the Boardwalk

47

HORIT PELED
Fall, Venice, California

PHILIP TAYLOR
At Rest, Billy Rose Sculpture Garden, Jerusalem

Hasidim
Raise up many disciples   Ethics of the Fathers 1:1

והעמידו תלמידים הרבה

ARTHUR Z. HERZIG
In Motion, Jerusalem

RHYNA GOLDSMITH
In Step, Jerusalem

HARRIET LEIBOWITZ
Strider, Jerusalem

SHEL ABELSON
Strollers

51

PHILIPPA GLAUBIGER
Lubavitcher Farbrengen, Brooklyn

RHODA MOGUL
Discussion

When I look at the world it sometimes seems to me as if every man were a tree in the wilderness, and God had no one in His world save man alone, and man had none he could turn to save God alone.   *Hasidic saying*

53

When a man is singing and cannot lift his voice, and another comes and sings with him—another who can lift his voice—the first will be able to lift his voice too. That is the secret of the bond between spirits. *Hasidic saying*

SY RUBIN
Discourse, the Lubavitcher Rebbe

CHANANYA KRONENBERG
Lag B'Omer Celebration, Israel

ANDREW PARTOS
Purim Feast, New Square, N. Y.

SHIMON MORALI
Meah Shearim

Trade

O prosper the work of our hands   Psalms 90:17

ומעשה ידינו כוננהו

BEA STADTLER
Shoemaker, Arab Market, Jerusalem

PHILIP TAYLOR
The Plasterer

58

Rabbi Kappara said: "Let a man always teach his son
a clean and easy handicraft."
    "What is such?"
Rabbi Judah answered: "Embroidery."

Babylonian Talmud, Kiddushin 82a

IRVING I. HERZBERG
Carpenter, Jaffa

BEA STADTLER
Reconstructing the Past

RICKI ROSEN
Alterations, New York City

LOUIS W. YOUNG
Retired Tailor, Bat Yam, Israel

JERRY STUART SILVERMAN
The Kerosene Seller, Acre

above right
ISAAC GELD
*Emergency Medical Service,
Williamsburg*

right
STEPHEN FOX
Fast Foods

STEPHEN FOX
The Mendel Weisberg Establishment, Essex Street

top
PETER A. COOPER
The Mendel Weisberg Establishment, Essex Street

above
GARY BIRNBAUM
The Mendel Weisberg Establishment, Essex Street

Shemaiah said: "A man must always love work and busy himself with it. For even of God to whom belongs the world and its fullness, it is written that 'He rested from all His work which He had done.'" *Avot de-Rabbi Nathan, XXI*

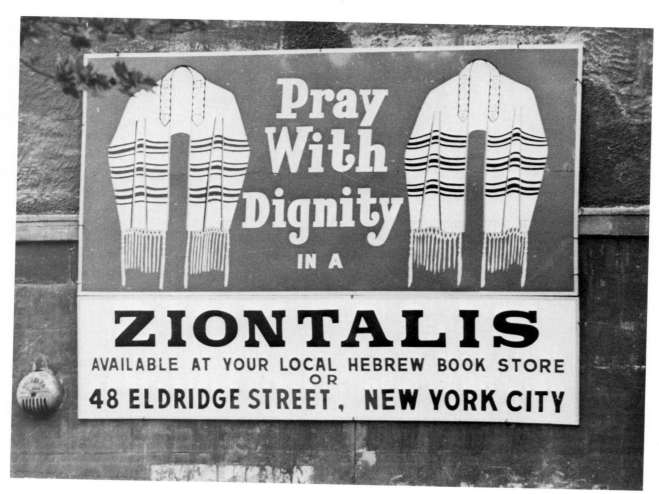

STEPHEN FOX
Billboard

BETTY H. ZOSS
Cordoba, 1976

PETER A. COOPER
Winter Night, Williamsburg

RITA PORETSKY
Countertop

STEPHEN FOX
Hair

RICHARD MARC SAKOLS
Canal Street

Indeed, the Lord your God has blessed you in all your undertakings.
Deuteronomy 2:7

JACK M. WHITE
Fairfax Avenue, Los Angeles

GARY BIRNBAUM
Pickle Stand, Lower East Side

STEPHEN FOX
Food Stop

RICHARD MARC SAKOLS
Hester Street

RITA CATHERINE GRECO
Harry Takes an Order, Pittsburgh

He who is about to pray should learn from the common laborer who sometimes takes a whole day to prepare a job. A wood-cutter who spends most of his day sharpening the saw and only the last hour cutting the wood has earned his day's wage.   Rabbi Mendel of Kotzk

ISAAC GELD
Sunday Afternoon, Lee Avenue, Brooklyn

RHYNA GOLDSMITH
Broom Seller, Jerusalem
HONORABLE MENTION

72

Food

When you have eaten your fill,
give thanks to the Lord   Deuteronomy 8:10

ואכלת ושבעת וברכת את ה' אלהיך

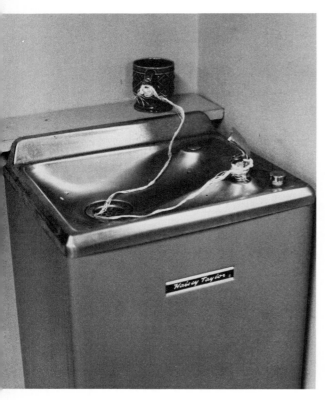

RICKI ROSEN
Yeshiva University Cafeteria

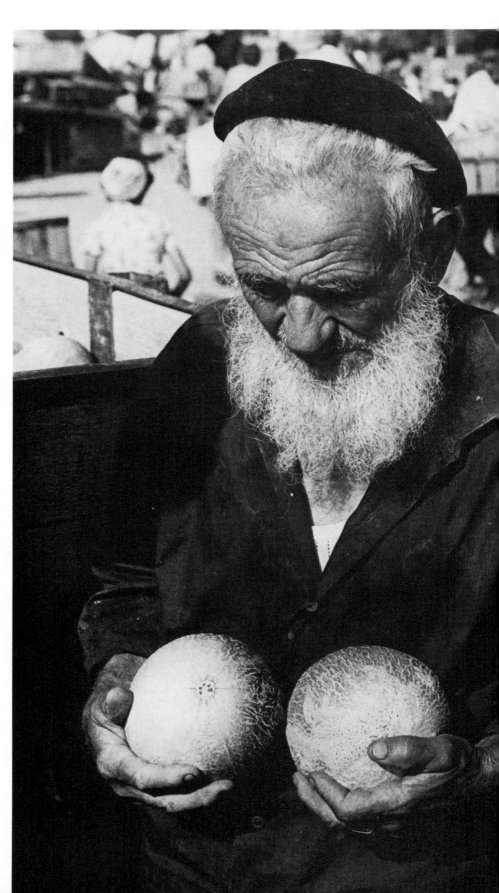

DAVID BEDEIN
Melon Buyer, Israel

74

ISAAC GELD
Mother's Hamantaschen

DEBRA APPLE
*Rachmiel and Jessica
Baking Hallah*

75

ISAAC GELD
Work Crew, Glatt Kosher Plant, Brooklyn

ROBERT M. KING
Chicken Flicker, London

What is profanation of the Name? Rav said, "I profane
it if I buy meat from the butcher and do not pay him
immediately." *Babylonian Talmud, Yoma 86a*

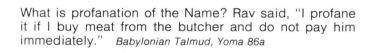

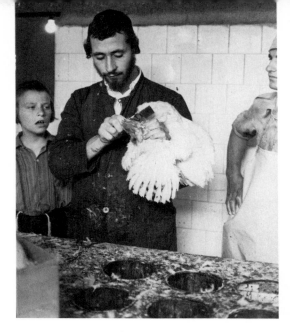

RITA CATHERINE GRECO
Sam the Butcher, Pittsburgh

ARTHUR Z. HERZIG
Shochet, Jerusalem

KAREN PLISKIN
Baking Matzot, Shiraz

SHEL ABELSON
Knish Vendor, Lower East Side

SY RUBIN
Knish Vendor, Lower East Side

Chew well with your teeth and you will feel it in your toes. *Babylonian Talmud, Shabbat 152a*

SURI LEVOW
Coca-Cola Truck, Israel

ISAAC GELD
The Driver

MITCHELL SMITH
Local Cafe, Tel Aviv

RICKI ROSEN
Cafeteria, Brighton Beach

ANDREW J. KLEINFELD
Felafel Stand, Agrippa Street, Jerusalem

MARK R. SIMON
Delancey Street Deli

JULIUS GINSBERG
L'chaim

It is cholent alone that unites them still in their old covenant.   Heinrich Heine

Demonstrations

Not by might, nor by power, but by My spirit

Zechariah 4:6

לא בחיל ולא בכח כי אם ברוחי

MORDECHAI MELES
Salute to Israel Parade, New York City
HONORABLE MENTION

GERALD LESTER
Showing the Flag

Where there is no peace, prayers are not heard.   Rabbi Nahman of Bratslav

MORDECHAI MELES
Marching for Peace

MORDECHAI MELES
Massed Flags

SHERRY SURIS
Hatikvah

89

GERALD LESTER
Israel Demonstration, Washington, D. C.

Elders sin by not protesting the sins of princes. *Babylonian Talmud, Shabbat 54a*

SHERRY SURIS
Rally, Foley Square, New York City

GERALD LESTER
Israel Demonstration, Washington, D. C.

ROSS COOPER
Rally, United Nations Plaza

HORIT PELED
Jewish Defense League, Los Angeles

HORIT PELED
Activists, Los Angeles

He who can protest and does not is an accomplice to the act. *Babylonian Talmud,*
Shabbat 54b

SY RUBIN
Remembering, Outdoor Observance, New York City

SY RUBIN
Spectators, Salute to Israel Parade, New York City

SYLVIA FRANKEL
Prayer and Deliverance

HORIT PELED
Supporting the Cause, Los Angeles

RIVKA SHIFMAN
"Let Our Brethren Go"

SY RUBIN
Solidarity in Protest

DEBORAH FRENKEL
Protest Posters, Paris

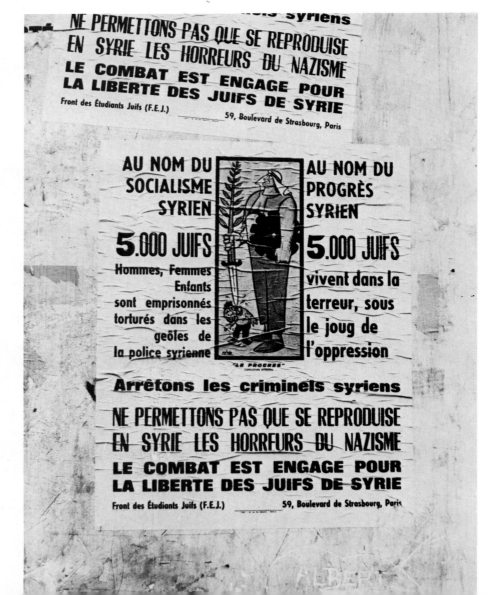

DEBORAH FRENKEL
Le Marais, Paris

99

DEBORAH FRENKEL
Le Marais, Paris

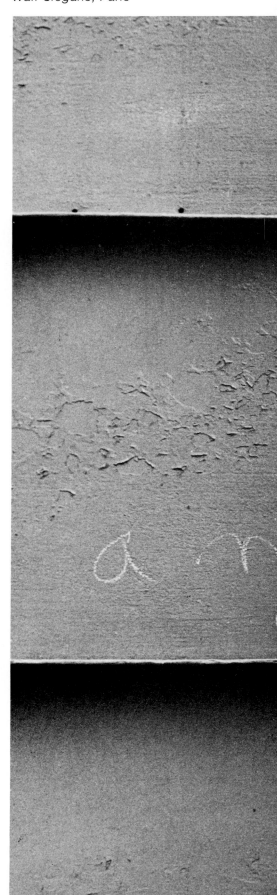

DEBORAH FRENKEL
Wall Slogans, Paris

Let all who work for the community do so for the sake of Heaven. *Ethics of the Fathers 2:2*

BILL ARON
Rally, New York City 1

BILL ARON
Rally, New York City 2

Cemeteries

These are the generations   Genesis 6:9

אלה תולדות

ZEVA OELBAUM
700-Year-Old Jewish Cemetery, Herat

MICHAEL ROSKIN
Jewish Cemetery, Prague

BELOVED MOTHER
FREIDA
SAMEL
DIED FEB. 6, 1931
AGE 75 YEARS

FRED ROSENBERG
Grove St. Cemetery, Newark

The day of death is concealed that man may build and plant.   *Midrash Tanhuma,*
Kedoshim 8

FRED ROSENBERG
Grove St. Cemetery, Newark

Glorified and sanctified be God's great name throughout the world which He has created according to His will. May He establish His kingdom hastening His salvation and the coming of His messiah, in your lifetime, during your days and within the life of all the house of Israel—speedily, soon, saying Amen.

May His great name be blessed forever and to eternity.

Blessed, praised, glorified, exalted, extolled, honored, adored, and lauded be the name of the Holy One, blessed be He, beyond all blessings and hymns, praises and consolations that are ever spoken in the world and say Amen.

May there be abundant peace from heaven, and a good life, for us and for all Israel, and say Amen.

He who creates peace in His celestial heights, may He create peace for us and for all Israel; and say Amen.   *Mourner's Kaddish*

FRED ROSENBERG
Grove St. Cemetery, Newark

KENNETH J. HILFMAN
Unveiling, Beth-El Cemetery, Paramus, N. J.

MICHAEL J. HOROWITZ
Desecrated Jewish Cemetery, Jerusalem

The deeper the sorrow, the less voice it has.   *Folksaying*

STANLEY BRATMAN
Waldheim Cemetery, Chicago

STANLEY BRATMAN
Waldheim Cemetery, Chicago

Holocaust

Remember what Amalek did to you
Deuteronomy 25:17

זכור את אשר עשה לך עמלק

STEPHEN EPSTEIN
The Gates of Hell, Auschwitz

He who kills an innocent person is responsible for the blood of all the victim's potential descendants, to the end of time.   *Mishnah, Sanhedrin 4:5*

KENNETH J. HILFMAN
Holocaust Memorial, Beth-El Cemetery, Paramus, N. J.

HARRIET LEIBOWITZ
Yad Vashem, Jerusalem

There are things which must cause you to lose your reason or you have none to lose.   Gotthold Ephraim Lessing

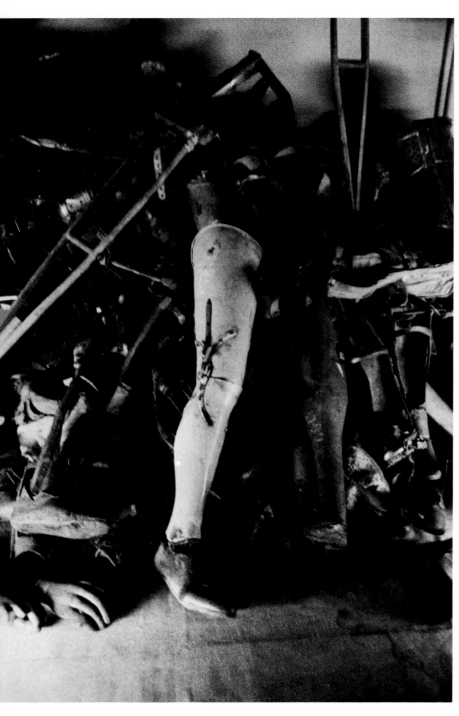

SY RUBIN
Artificial Limbs, Maidanek

STEPHEN EPSTEIN
Auschwitz

People

C-d

Partnership

בין אדם למקום

Weddings
The voice of joy and gladness
From the blessings of the marriage service

קול ששון וקול שמחה

preceding pages
JULIUS GINSBERG
Rabbi's Instruction

ISAAC GELD
Bride

IRVING I. HERZBERG
Under the Huppah

ANDREW PARTOS
Father and Bride

ANDREW PARTOS
Bride and Groom

HELENE RYESKY
Wedding Toast

SUSAN MOGUL
Father of the Bride

WARREN SOLODAR
Reading the Ketubah,
Russian Immigrant Absorption Center, Beersheba

WARREN SOLODAR
Signing the Marriage Contract, Kibbutz Shefayim

SHERRY SURIS
Hasidic Wedding

SHERRY SURIS
Across the Mehizah

From every human being there rises a light that reaches straight to heaven. And when two souls that are destined to be together find each other, their streams of light flow together, and a single brighter light goes forth from their united being.   Israel Baal Shem Tov

Entering the Covenant

He is ever mindful of His covenant   Psalms 105:8

זכר לעולם בריתו

May God bless this tender child of eight days;
may his hands and heart be firm with God.
From the special prayer after the meal at a brit

SHERRY SURIS
Under the Wimpel

WARREN SOLODAR
Brit Milah, Beersheba

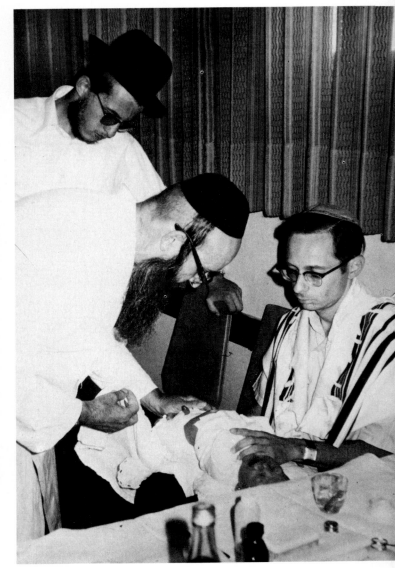

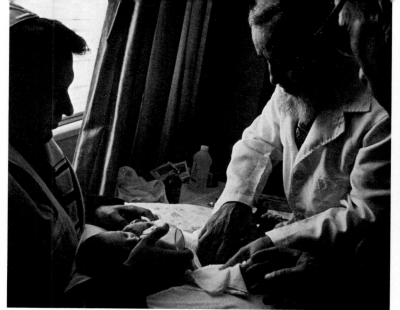

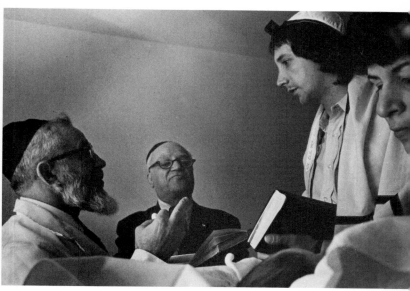

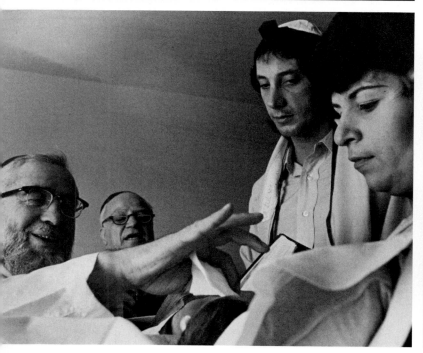

JOSHUA SIDEROWITZ
Sephardic Brit

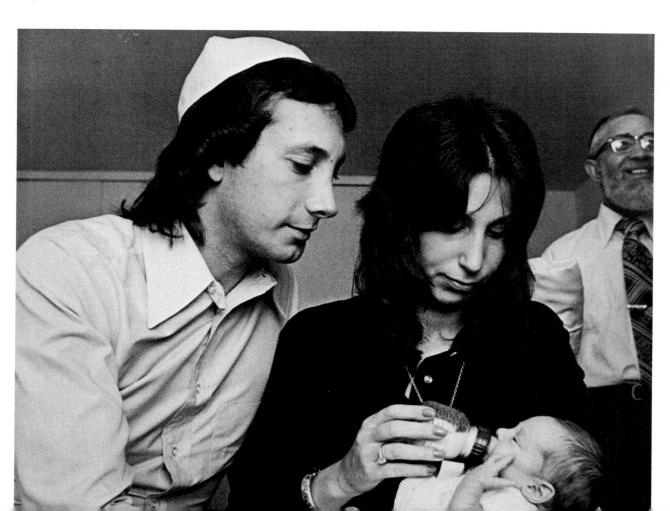

129

Bar / Bat Mitzvah

He shall reconcile fathers with sons
and sons with their fathers   Malachi 3:24

והשיב לב אבות על בנים
ולב בנים על אבותם

SUSAN MOGUL
Jess

IRVING I. HERZBERG
Reading the Torah

130

AVI FISHMAN
Bar Mitzvah Joy

Prayer

In distress I called on the Lord   Psalms 118:5

מן המצר קראתי יה

Let your prayer be a window to Heaven.   Israel Baal Shem Tov

SY RUBIN
Lubavitch Synagogue, Brooklyn

SHARON SAUERHOFF
Yom Kippur, Attorney Street Synagogue, New York City

JERRY SILVER
Shavuot Service, Fabrangen, Washington

134

BILL ARON
Shavuot, New York Havurah

A man needs no fixed place to say his prayers, no synagogue.
Among the trees of the forest, everywhere one can pray.   Israel Baal Shem Tov

PHILIP TAYLOR
Erev Shabbat, Jerusalem

It would be better for every man to pray when he feels inspired, to pray his own prayer and in a language familiar to him.   Rabbi Nahman of Bratslav

IRVING I. HERZBERG
Prayer at the Wall

DOROTHY HARWOOD
Morning Prayer

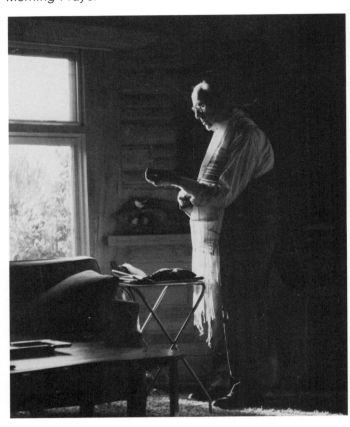

138

ALVIN SILBERMAN
East End Synagogue, Long Beach, N. Y.

DENNIS BRISKIN
Reciting Psalms, Israel

WALTER RABETZ
Solitary Prayer

GABRIELA J. LANDAU
Studying the Torah Portion

Tefillin

Bind them as a sign   Deuteronomy 6:8

וקשרתם לאות על ידך

NEIL WALDEN
Fairfax, Los Angeles

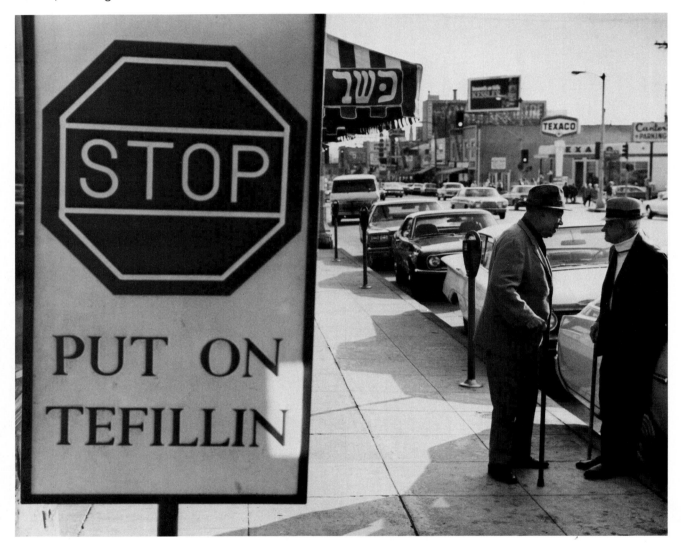

Lord of the Universe! I saw an ordinary Jew pick up his tefillin from the floor
and kiss them; and You have let Your tefillin—the Jewish people—lie on the
ground for more than two thousand years, trampled by their enemies! Why do
You not act as a simple Jew acts? Why?   Rabbi Levi Yitzhak of Berditchev

ROBERT M. KING
Mitzvah at the Wall

When a person puts on the tefillin of the hand, he should stretch out his left arm as though to draw to him the Community of Israel and to embrace her with his right arm.   *Zohar*

142

ALVIN SILBERMAN
Shaharit, Long Beach, N. Y.

MAXINE MARGULIES
The Tefillin Lesson, Germantown Jewish Center, Philadelphia

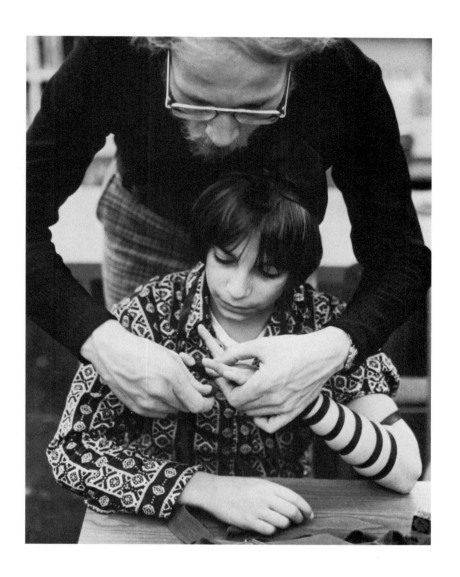

JOAN BEDER
Devotional, Jerusalem

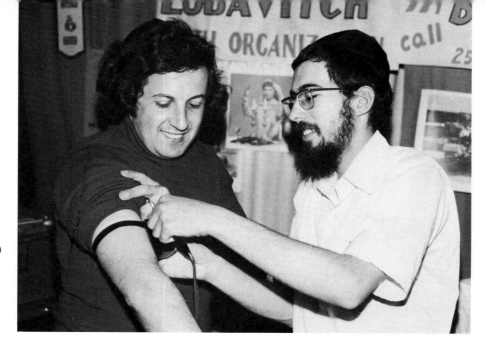

JULIUS SEEWALD
*Lubavitch Tefillin Campaign,
New York City 1*

JULIUS SEEWALD
*Lubavitch Tefillin Campaign,
New York City 2*

STANLEY NEWFIELD
Ba'al Tefillah, Brooklyn

Study

For they are our life and the length of our days
Ahavat Olam prayer

כי הם חיינו ואֹרך ימינו

MYRA ALPERSON
Yeshivas, Lower East Side

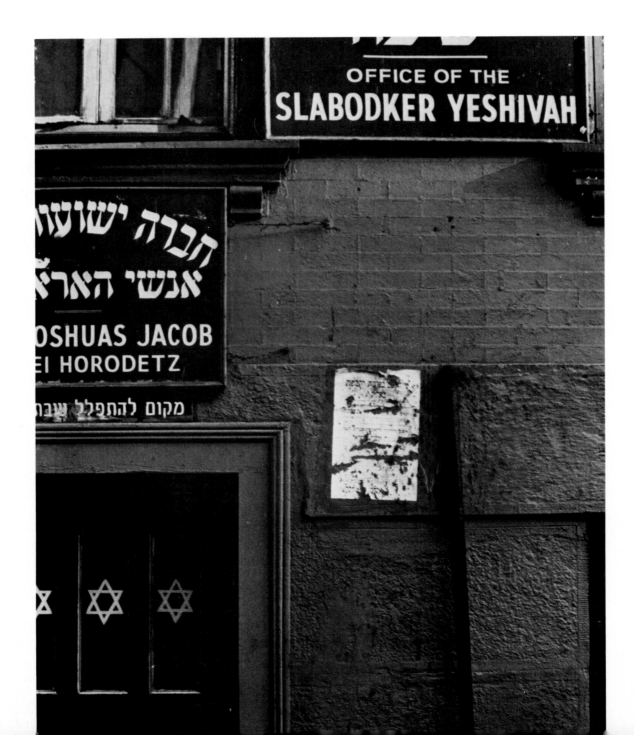

146

A RECENT IMMIGRANT COMES
FROM THE SOVIET UNION
TO HIS FAMILY IN THE U.S.

and asks
      3 questions in shul:
                        1. Where
      are the children?
                        2. Where
      are the children?
                        3. Where
      are the children?

Did I pass through Auschwitz
      to see a synagogue
      too dignified to tolerate
      five-year-olds playing on the bima?
Did I live in Leningrad
      for 30 years
      at minyans for the feeble zeydehs
  to find a freedom
      empty of the noise
      of unadulterated childhood?
There they hid or died.
There their parents' fear
      turned them into goyim
      and marranos
But here there is no reason.
Without giggling and shouts
      and infants crying
      your sanctuary
      is a vacant temple
      your prayers
      are hypocritical.
  Let us have noise and chaos
in the house of prayer
  Lest we cause ourselves
a self-made holocaust
  Lest Berlin and Moscow
win a victory
  we fought
  but lose now
for the sake
  of order
  and a myth of church-learned
      straight proprieties

            Daniel Siegel, *And God Braided Eve's Hair*

BILL ARON
New York Havurah School
SECOND PRIZE

SHELDON MOSKOWITZ
Shabbat Lesson

HAROLD S. SOLOMON
Outdoor Study, Safed

RHODA MOGUL
Learning, Israel

ALEX MERMEL
Studying the Haggadah

ARNOLD J. PAKULA
Talmud Student, Miami Beach

ALVIN SILBERMAN
Pondering the Question

MICHAEL SPIER
Transmitting the Tradition

IRVING I. HERZBERG
Book Store, Williamsburg

GERALD MILLMAN
Young Scribe

152

far left
SHELDON MOSKOWITZ
Workbook

left
GERALD MILLMAN
Aleph-Beth

God loves two students who arrange to study together.   Rabbi Simeon ben Lakish

Torah

It is a tree of life   Proverbs 3:18

עֵץ חַיִּים הִיא

The Torah was not written in ink nor was it engraved on stone. It was white fire
carved on black fire.   Joseph Opatashu

CAROL BLOOM
Sephardic Torah

STEVEN ZUCKER
Sofer,
Commack, N. Y.

N. J. RIEUR
Writing the Torah,
East Brunswick, N. J.

STANLEY NEWFIELD
Reciting the Torah Blessings

STANLEY NEWFIELD
Reading the Torah

STANLEY NEWFIELD
Hagbah

156

MARK R. SIMON
*Sabbath Service,
Maplewood, N. J.*

Every glory and wonder, every deep mystery and all beautiful wisdom are hidden in the Torah—sealed up in her treasures.   Nahmanides

AVI FISHMAN
Scroll at the Wall

157

ELAINE A. PIPE
Siyum Hatorah, Haddon Heights, N. J.

The religion of the Torah learned to do without the Temple, but it never dreamed
of doing without the synagogue.   Robert Travers Herford

ROSS COOPER
Simhat Torah

GERALD MILLMAN
Cantor, Temple Sinai, Amityville, N. Y.

ALVIN SILBERMAN
Parokhet, Long Beach, N.Y.

JOSEPH L. PODOLSKY
*Junior Congregation,
Palo Alto*

Synagogues
To live in the House of the Lord   Psalms 27:4

שבתי בבית ה׳

Don't wreck the old synagogue before you build the new.   *Babylonian Talmud, Baba Bathra 3b*

SUELLEN SNYDER
Zitomer Yeshiva,
New York City,
Stripped Interior
FIRST   PRIZE

DEBORAH FRENKEL
Synagogue, Paris

SUELLEN SNYDER
Anshe Slonim,
Norfolk Street,
Oldest Synagogue
in New York City

160

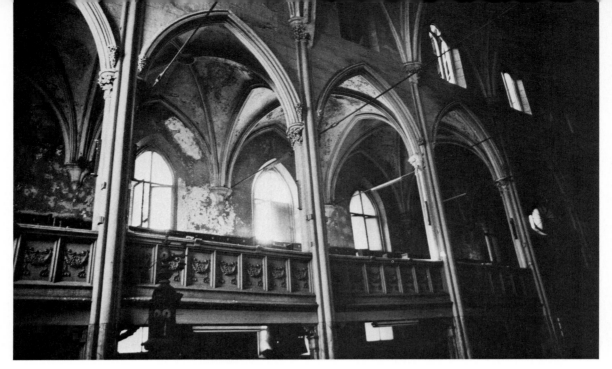

SUELLEN SNYDER
Anshe Slonim, Norfolk Street, New York City

SUELLEN SNYDER
Warsaw Synagogue, Rivington Street, New York City

SUELLEN SNYDER
Mahover Synagogue,
Henry Street,
New York City,
Charred Interior

SUELLEN SNYDER
Warsaw Synagogue, Rivington Street, New York City

SUELLEN SNYDER
*Mahover Synagogue, Henry Street,
New York City, Charred Interior*

Jews may not enlarge, elevate, or beautify their synagogues.   Alfonso X

163

RITA PORETSKY
Former Synagogue

ISAAC GELD
Former Synagogue

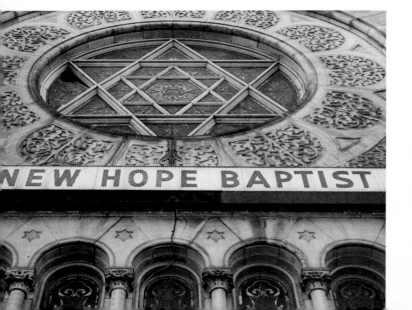

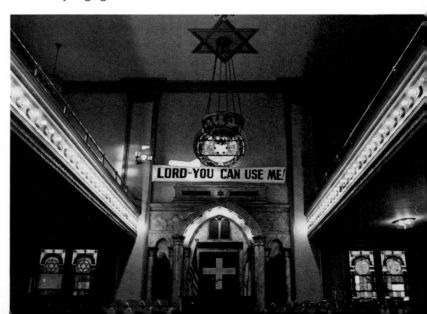

SY RUBIN
Synagogue President, Warsaw

MYRA ALPERSON
Synagogue Facade, Lower East Side

RITA PORETSKY
Former Synagogue

ISAAC GELD
Former Synagogue
HONORABLE MENTION

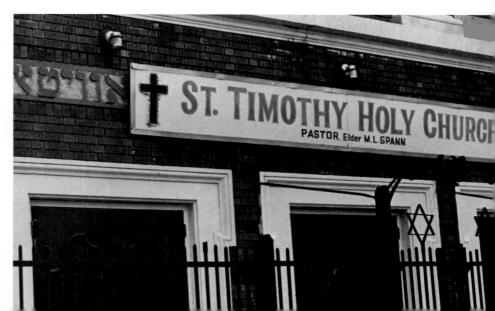

Shabbat

Remember the Sabbath day and keep it holy
Exodus 20:8

זכור את יום השבת לקדשו

It is said that on the eve of the Sabbath two ministering angels accompany a man from the synagogue to his home. If, when he arrives home, he finds the candles burning, the table laid, and the couch covered with a spread, the good angel declares, "May it be thus on another Sabbath too," and the evil angel is obliged to answer, "Amen." But if not, the evil angel declares, "May it be thus on another Sabbath too," and the good angel is obliged to answer, "Amen." *Babylonian Talmud, Shabbat 119b*

IRVING I. HERZBERG
Sabbath Candles

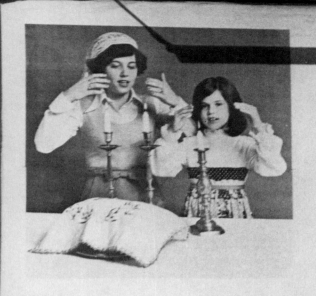

Get Chai.
Light Shabbos
Candles.

Chabad House: 477-8647

Design courtesy of Lerner Newhoff Advertising. Photography: Joel Nussbaum

A FOSTER AND KLEISER PUBLIC SERVICE MESSAGE

Every seventh day a miracle comes to pass—the resurrection of the soul, of the soul of man and of the soul of all things.   Abraham Joshua Heschel, *The Sabbath*

GERALD MILLMAN
Friday Night Services, Massapequa, N. Y.

HERBERT A. CHESLER
"L'hadlik Ner Shel Shabbat,"
First-Grade Sunday School, Pittsburgh

ALEX MERMEL
Billboard, Fairfax Avenue, Los Angeles

Come my beloved to meet the Bride.
Let us welcome the presence of the Sabbath.
Come in peace . . . and come in joy . . .
Come O Bride! Come O Bride!   *Lekha Dodi prayer*

GABRIELA J. LANDAU
Sabbath Lights

Holidays

You shall rejoice in your festival   Deuteronomy 16:14

ושמחת בחגך

IRVING I. HERZBERG
Hanukkah Candles
THIRD PRIZE

FRED H. STEIGER
The Hanukkah Gift

The Hasmoneans entered the sanctuary, rebuilt the gates, closed the breaches, and cleansed the Temple court from the slain and the impurities. They looked for pure olive oil to light the Menorah and found only one bottle with the seal of the high priest so that they were sure of its purity. Though its quantity seemed sufficient for only one day's lighting, it lasted for eight days. . . . Hence the Hasmoneans and all the Jews instituted these eight days as a time of feasting and rejoicing . . . and so the Jews everywhere observe this festival for eight days. . . . These days, instituted by the priests, Levites, and the sages of the Temple shall be celebrated by their descendants forever. *The Scroll of Hasmoneans, 68-76*

FRED H. STEIGER
Hanukkah Lights

FRED H. STEIGER
Hanukkah Lights

GABRIELA LANDAU
Hanukkah Lights

JACK LEVY
Hanukkah Lights

JUDAH MINTZ
Hanukkah Lights

SIDNEY HECKER
Hanukkah Lights

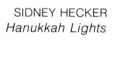

SY RUBIN
Purim Masquerade, Brooklyn
HONORABLE MENTION

MORRIS M. FAIERSTEIN
Purim Masquerade, Jerusalem

MORRIS M. FAIERSTEIN
Purim Masquerade, Jerusalem

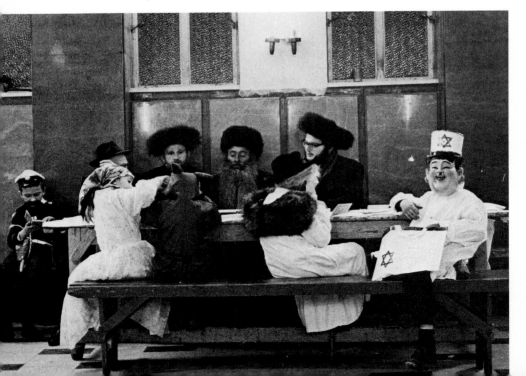

IRVING I. HERZBERG
Purim Masquerade, Brooklyn

On Purim one should drink until he cannot tell the difference between "Cursed be Haman!" and "Blessed be Mordecai!"   *Babylonian Talmud, Megillah 7b*

MORRIS M. FAIERSTEIN
Purim Masquerade, Jerusalem

175

ETHEL DIAMOND
Family Seder

Why is this night different from all other nights? *Passover Haggadah*

ARTHUR Z. HERZIG
Sukkot Scene, Jerusalem

HERBERT A. CHESLER
Lubavitch Sukkah Mobile, Pittsburgh

JOSEPH L. PODOLSKY
Model Seder, Palo Alto

HELEN RYESKY
Lulav and Etrog

GABRIELA J. LANDAU
Sukkot Series

BILL ARON
Harvest

SOL GENUTH
Erev Sukkot, Canal Street

SOL GENUTH
Preparing for Sukkot, Canal Street

You shall take the fruit of *hadar* trees, branches of palm trees, bows of leafy trees, and willows of the brook, and you shall rejoice before the Lord your God seven days.   *Leviticus 23:40*

"THIS *ETROG* IS AN *ETROG*"

The wise men of Helm were elated with the *etrog* the president of their congregation had purchased for Sukkot. This was not an ordinary *etrog*. It came from the Land of Israel. It was yellow as the color of an *etrog*. It was fragrant as the odor of an *etrog*. It was without a blemish as an *etrog*. It had a firm and dainty *pitma*. In short, this was an *etrog*!

The president reluctantly entrusted the sexton to take the *etrog* to all the Helm householders so that they could recite the traditional blessing over it. Apprehensive of the sexton's carelessness, the president warned him:

"Remember! This *etrog* is an *etrog*! Handle it with tenderness. Be especially careful that the *pitma* should not be spoiled by handling and thereby render the *etrog* unsuitable for use. Remember! This *etrog* is an *etrog*."

The wise sexton joyfully embarked on his holy mission. Clutching the *etrog* in both hands, he started out through the streets of Helm, when a sudden inspiration stopped him in his tracks. He looked at the *etrog*, held it level with his eyes, and scrutinized it from all sides. Shutting his eyes in devout meditation, the sexton recalled the president's instructions to take extreme precautions that the *pitma* should not be spoiled. Ah, he was shrewd! But what was the inspiration that brought him to a sudden halt? Had he forgotten his clever device? No! No! He knew what he had to do. No sooner said than done!

The sexton took a sharp knife from his pocket and carefully cut out the *pitma* from the *etrog*. The president had ordered him to take good care of it, and he would never dare disobey the president. He wrapped the *pitma* in a clean handkerchief and gently placed it in his pocket. He then proceeded to the homes of the wise Helmites to allow them to recite the blessing over the *etrog*.

As the sexton entered each home, he reiterated the president's admonition:

"Remember! This *etrog* is an *etrog*!"   Helm tale

RIVKA SHIFMAN
The Proper Selection, Canal Street

IRVING I. HERZBERG
Simhat Torah Celebration, Brooklyn

STANLEY BRATMAN
Flag Seller

top
BILL ARON
Simhat Torah, New York City 1

above
BILL ARON
Simhat Torah, New York City 2

Israel, the Land

ישראל

Arrival

This is the land of which I swore
to Abraham, Isaac, and Jacob,
"I will give it to your offspring"
Deuteronomy 34:4

זאת הארץ אשר נשבעתי
לאברהם ליצחק וליעקב לאמר
לזרעך אתננה

WARREN SOLODAR
View of Haifa

preceding pages
SURI LEVOW
A New Generation

No matter where I go it is always to Israel.   Rabbi Nahman of Bratslav

ROBERT M. KING
Homeward Bound, Kennedy Airport

188

Life

Walk around Zion, circle it   Psalms 48:13

סבו ציון והקיפוה

PHILIP TAYLOR
Erev Shabbat, Meah Shearim

ABRAHAM A. DAVIDSON
Interior, Meah Shearim

ANDREW J. KLEINFELD
Mahane Yehudah, Jerusalem

RHODA MOGUL
Shalom!

WALTER RABETZ
At Ease in Zion

192

Our God in Heaven, bless the State of Israel . . . shield it beneath the wings of Your love; spread over it the canopy of Your peace; send Your light and Your truth to its leaders and direct them with Your good counsel. . . . Establish peace in the land and everlasting joy for its inhabitants. *Prayer for the State of Israel*

JOAN BEDER
Arab Women, Jerusalem

DENNIS BRISKIN
Two Worlds

CHANANYA KRONENBERG
Lag B'Omer, Meron

SURI LEVOW
Jerusalem Passage

194

SYLVIA VEGA-ORTIZ
Sinai Oasis

ISAAC GELD
Grandmother and Grandchild, Meron

195

I will make of you a great nation. *Genesis 12:2*

PHILIP TAYLOR
Helmsman, Eilat

IRVING I. HERZBERG
Children, Meah Shearim

SYLVIA VEGA-ORTIZ
Children, Haifa

GEORGE HOLZ
Trio, Jerusalem

PHILIP TAYLOR
On the Beach, Tel Aviv

Marketplace

Thus Israel dwells in safety . . .
in a land of grain and wine,
under heavens dripping dew

Deuteronomy 33:28

וישכן ישראל בטח...
אל ארץ דגן ותירוש
אף שמיו יערפו טל

No scholar should live in a town where vegetables are unobtainable.   *Babylonian Talmud, Erubin 55b*

DAVID BEDEIN
Doing the Marketing

ARTHUR Z. HERZIG
Last Produce, Meah Shearim

ARTHUR Z. HERZIG
Market Day, Meah Shearim

201

RHODA MOGUL
Marketplace

False scales are an abomination to the Lord; but a just weight is his delight.
Proverbs 11:1

ANDREW J. KLEINFELD
Street Stall

RHODA MOGUL
Street Stall

To be a successful businessman you need extraordinary talents; and if you have such talents, why waste them on business?   Rabbi Israel Salanter Lipkin

Graffiti

Mutter upon mutter, murmur upon murmur
Isaiah 28:13

צו לצו צו לצו קו לקו קו לקו

RHODA MOGUL
Community Notices

HAROLD S. SOLOMON
Message, Old City, Jerusalem

HEBREW

I'll tell you how much I love Hebrew:
Read me anything—
        Genesis
        or an ad in an Israeli paper
and watch my face.
I will make half-sounds of ecstasy
and my smile will be so enormously sweet
you would think some angels were singing Psalms
        or God Himself was reciting to me.
I am crazy for her Holiness
        and each restaurant's menu in Yerushalayim
        or Bialik poem
gives me peace no Dante or Milton or Goethe
could give.
I have heard Iliads of poetry,
Omar Khayyam in Farsi,
and Virgil sung as if the poet himself
were coaching the reader.
And they move me—
but not like
the train schedule from Haifa to Tel Aviv
or a choppy unsyntaxed note
from a student who got half the grammar I taught him
        all wrong
but remembered to write
    with Alefs and Zayins and Shins.
That's the way I am.
I'd rather hear the weather report
on Kol Yisrael
than all the rhythms and music of Shakespeare.

Daniel Siegel, *And God Braided Eve's Hair*

207

SHEL ABELSON
Wall Scrawls

GEORGE HOLZ
Protest of the Faithful

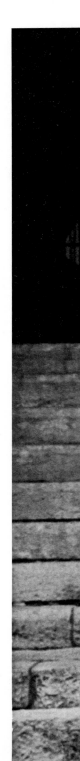

RHODA MOGUL
Communication

Oh Lord, open my lips.   *Psalms 51:17*

The Wall

These shall stand as a testimony to the Lord,
as an everlasting sign that shall not perish   Isaiah 55:13

והיה לה' לשם
לאות עולם לא יכרת

SHEL ABELSON
Aliyat Regel

210

The Wall . . . At first I am stunned. Then I see: a Wall of frozen tears, a cloud of sighs.

Palimpsests, hiding books, secret names. The stones are seals.

The Wall . . . The old mother crying for all of us. Stubborn, loving, waiting for redemption. The ground on which I stand is Amen. My words become echoes. All of our history is waiting here. Abraham Joshua Heschel, *Israel: An Echo of Eternity*

SURI LEVOW
Approaching the Wall

Your name shall no longer be Jacob, but Israel, for you have striven with beings divine and human, and have prevailed.   *Genesis 32:29*

FREYA OPPER
Contemplation

KIVA SHTULL
Minyan

KIVA SHTULL
Washing the Hands

MORDECHAI MELES
Prayer in the Rain

MARK R. SIMON
Informal Prayer

For the sake of the Unity of the Holy One, with reverence and love, in complete unity with all Israel, I enwrap myself in the fringed garment. May my soul and body also be enveloped—in the light of the tzitzit which encompass all six hundred and thirteen mitzvot. As I cover myself with a tallit of this world, may I deserve to be robed in a dignified garment and a beautiful tallit in the world to come. By virtue of the tzitzit may my soul and may my prayer escape the danger of the profane. May the tallit symbolically spread its sheltering wings over my soul and over my prayer "like an eagle that stirs its nestlings, fluttering over its young." *Prayer on donning the tallit*

JOAN BEDER
Davening

IRVING I. HERZBERG
Petitioner

215

WALTER RABETZ
Solitude

If I knew that I had answered a single "Amen" as it ought to be said, I would be contented.   Rabbi Moses of Kobrin

KIVA SHTULL
Solitude

RICHARD TRACHTENBERG
Solitude

WALTER RABETZ
Solitude

Remembrance

He who dies at a hundred years shall
be reckoned a youth
Isaiah 65:20

כי הנער בן מאה שנה ימות

CARL A. BIANCO
Caskets, Sinai
HONORABLE MENTION

SHERRY SURIS
*Munich Massacre Burials,
Har Hamenuhot, Jerusalem*

All my sleep had fled because of the bitterness of my soul.   *Isaiah 38:15*

Guardians of Israel

Pray for the well-being of Jerusalem;
may those who love you be at peace
Psalms 122:6

שאלו שלום ירושלים ישליו אהביך

When men war, God's anger does not frighten them.   *Zohar*

JOAN BEDER
On Leave

GEORGE HOLZ
Golan Heights

IRVING I. HERZBERG
Knesset Guards

DEBORAH FRENKEL
Soldier

HARRIET LIEBOWITZ
Soldier

GEORGE HOLZ
Soldier

ADAM BARUCH LAIPSON
"The Tower," Sculpture by Kenneth Snelson,
Hirshhorn Museum, Washington
HONORABLE MENTION

Where there is no vision, the people perish.   *Proverbs 29:18*